To ....

From ....

Date ....

Prayers of Promise: Praying God's Life-Changing Promises Over Your Children
Copyright © 2017 by Roy Lessin
ISBN: 978-1-68408-138-7

Published by:

DaySpring

P.O. Box 1010
Siloam Springs, AR 72761
www.dayspring.com

PRAYERS

— of —

PROMISE

God's Life-Changing Promises to Pray over Your Children

ROY LESSIN

Dedicated to my father, Joseph Aaron Lessin,
who faithfully prayed for me for more than
forty-five years and left me a spiritual heritage
for which I am eternally grateful.

PRAYERS
—of—
PROMISE

*God's Life-Changing Promises
to Pray over Your Children*

*Parents and grandparents have been given
two great privileges...
the first is to talk to their children and
grandchildren about the Lord, and
the second is to talk to the Lord about
their children and grandchildren.*
—Roy Lessin

How to Use this Book

We desire that as you use this book your prayers will
be led of the Lord. Some may be led to go through the
book in the order the prayers appear, others may move
from place to place as they focus their prayers on certain
specific needs. Each prayer is appropriate to pray over
children at any stage or age in life, and will help you
build a foundation of prayer to last a lifetime.

For your convenience and ease of use, a table of contents
has been provided. The book has been divided into ten
sections. Each section includes six prayers and promises
that focus on a specific heartfelt need within the life of a
child. Each section ends with *At the Heart of the Prayer*,
featuring a key focal point from each prayer.

Each prayer is based upon the promises of God. This is
important for our faith, because it assures us that we
are praying in agreement with God's will. Consider

these amazing, faith-strengthening words from the book of I John:

> *This is the confidence (the assurance, the privilege of boldness) which we have in Him: [we are sure] that if we ask anything (make any request) according to His will (in agreement with His own plan), He listens to and hears us. And if (since) we [positively] know that He listens to us in whatever we ask, we also know [with settled and absolute knowledge] that we have [granted us as our present possessions] the requests made of Him.*
> I John 5:14–15 AMP

God bless you as you pray.

A mother who is praying for her children shared the following ways she has used this book.

This book of prayers has helped me:
- *Pray using Scripture.*
- *Find words that really pray what I'm thinking.*
- *Have a tool to encourage me to be structured in my prayers, yet creative in how I pray.*
- *Remember that my children are never too old to need my prayers.*
- *Find other moms to pray with so we can encourage each other.*

Table of Contents

Section One

THE POWER OF BLESSING

The Power of Blessing

He [Jesus] took the children in his arms and placed his
hands on their heads and blessed them.
Mark 10:16 NLT

God loves to bless the lives of children, and parents have the awesome privilege of extending the blessing of God to each child. Your words speak the blessing of God, your hands impart the blessing of God, and your heart express the blessing of God. As you ask God to bless your children, you are asking for His best, His highest, and His greatest good for their lives.

Children grow and thrive under the blessing of God. As you bless your children, they will hear words of hope, encouragement, and support. Prayers of blessing will build them up rather than beat them down; heal them rather than hurt them; strengthen them rather than weaken them; and help them follow the good God has for their lives rather than lead them astray.

This section's promises focus on the following needs:

Learning God's Voice

Nearness

Meaning and Purpose

Freedom

Strength

Victory

Learning God's Voice

Promise

*"All your children shall be taught by the LORD, and
great shall be the peace of your children... No weapon
formed against you shall prosper, and every tongue
which rises against you in judgment You shall condemn.
This is the heritage of the servants of the LORD, and their
righteousness is from Me," says the LORD.*

Isaiah 54:13,17 NKJV

Prayer

Lord, I pray that each of my children will be taught by You. Be their teacher, instructor, and guide. Teach them how to walk with You and learn from You. I pray that, above all, they will always know Your wisdom and Your ways. May they learn of You, see You, know You, and love You.

Above all voices, may they hear Your voice; above all pathways, may they know Your ways; above all advice, may they learn Your counsel; above all knowledge, may they have Your understanding; above all opinions, may they have Your wisdom.

I also ask that Your peace will be their peace; Your peace will cover them and keep them; Your peace will guard their hearts and minds. I ask that they will have peaceful thoughts and walk in the ways of peace.

Nearness

Promise

I will establish My covenant between Me and you and your descendants after you throughout their generations for an everlasting covenant, to be God to you and to your descendants after you. I will give to you and to your descendants after you the land in which you are a stranger [moving from place to place], all the land of Canaan, as an everlasting possession [of property]; and I will be their God.

Genesis 17:-7–8 AMP

Prayer

Father, according to Your covenant promise to Abraham, assuring us that You will always be our God and the God of our children, I ask You to reveal Yourself to the hearts of my children and fulfill Your covenant promises to them.

You are faithful to every generation that loves You and puts their trust in You. I thank You that You have shown Your faithfulness to generations past in countless ways and at countless times; You have shown Your faithfulness to me, in my generation; and You will show Yourself faithful to the generation to come.

I thank You that I can put my complete trust in You to be my children's God at all times and in all ways. Be their God in their going out and coming in, their life choices and decisions, their waiting times and busy times, their happy times and times of sorrow, their times of testing and times of celebration. I know this to be true, because You are always true to Your promises. My children will always find You faithful as they put their trust in You.

Meaning and Purpose

Promise

They will not build and another occupy; they will not plant and another eat [the fruit]. For as the lifetime of a tree, so will be the days of My people, and My chosen [people] will fully enjoy [and long make use of] the work of their hands. They will not labor in vain, or bear children for disaster; for they are the descendants of those blessed by the Lord, and their offspring with them.

Isaiah 65:22–23 AMP

Prayer

Lord, I'm so grateful that we belong to You. You have saved us from a life of emptiness—empty words, empty promises, empty desires, empty thoughts, empty goals, empty work, and empty choices. Your life has freed us, as a family, from empty relationships with each other.

Thank You for Your grace, Your power, and Your love. Thank You for Your promise that we will not face a hopeless, worthless, and meaningless future. I believe we have been brought into this world for redemption rather than destruction, peace rather than panic, completeness rather than emptiness, and the glorification of Your name rather than frustration.

Thank You, Father, for the blessings that You have extended to me and my family. I know that in every circumstance of life, You are working all things together for our good and to fulfill Your purposes.

Freedom

Promise

The Lord who made you and helps you says:
Do not be afraid, O Jacob, my servant, O dear Israel,
my chosen one. For I will pour out water to quench your
thirst and to irrigate your parched fields.
And I will pour out my Spirit on your descendants,
and my blessing on your children.

Isaiah 44:2–4 NLT

Prayer

My Father, what a wonderful God You are. You have made my children by hand. You are their Designer as well as their Helper and Keeper. I ask that they will never doubt, question, or wonder who they are, where they came from, or where they are going.

May they live free of fear—safe from its bondage, kept from its paralyzing grip, and protected from everything that would terrify them. Keep them free from anything that would hinder them as they seek to experience Your perfect plan for their lives. May their hearts be full of expectancy and assurance, knowing that You have set them free.

Pour out upon each child, Your abundant mercies, Your abundant grace, Your abundant goodness, Your abundant blessings, and Your abundant love. May they always drink from Your fountain of joy, wash in the river of Your mercies, and be touched by Your refreshing rains. Quench their thirsty souls, water the garden of their hearts, and keep their spirits in Your healing streams. Cause them to thrive, flourish, and prosper in life and in each of their relationships with You.

Strength

Promise

I love You, L<small>ORD</small>; You are my strength.
The L<small>ORD</small> is my rock, my fortress, and my savior;
my God is my rock, in whom I find protection.
He is my shield, the power that saves me,
and my place of safety.

Psalm 18:1–2 NLT

Prayer

Almighty God, You are the Mighty Warrior. You are our strength. You have all power! You are the Omnipotent One, the God of Majesty, the God of Truth, the God of Every Victory. I'm thankful that Your promises can be completely trusted. Your throne is in the heavens, and Your rule and reign is over all.

May my children look to You, trust in You, and lean upon Your resources every moment of every day. When facing temptation, make them strong to resist. Give them the strength to say no to everything that would draw them away from You and yes to everything that will draw them closer to Your heart.

When they are facing lies, protect their minds with the shield of Your powerful truth. When they are facing deception, keep their feet on Your pathway of righteousness and peace. When they are facing false accusations, draw close to them with Your all-encompassing, all-embracing love.

Victory

Promise

Give all your worries and cares to God,
for He cares about you. Stay alert!
Watch out for your great enemy, the devil.
He prowls around like a roaring lion,
looking for someone to devour.

Stand firm against him,
and be strong in your faith.
Remember that your Christian brothers and sisters
all over the world are going through
the same kind of suffering you are.

I Peter 5:7–9 NLT

Prayer

Lord, according to Your Word, we have an enemy who wants to rob us, kill us, and destroy our faith and trust in You. I thank You that what You seek to do in our lives is more powerful than what the enemy seeks to do. I'm thankful that You are greater than anything or anyone who would come against us.

Father, may Your truth always keep our children from Satan's lies; may Your light always keep them from his darkness; may Your wisdom always keep them from his confusion; may Your peace always keep them from his restlessness; and may Your pathway always keep them from his dead-end road.

Give my children grace enough to cast all their worries and cares upon You, rather than being weighed down with concerns that You never intended for them to carry. By Your grace, help my children stand firm against every scheme of the devil, grow stronger each day in their faith and confidence in You, and pray for others with a sincere heart of love and understanding.

At the Heart of the Prayer

A key focus of each prayer to carry in your heart.

Learning God's Voice

Above all voices, may they hear Your voice; above all pathways, may they know Your ways; above all advice, may they learn Your counsel; above all knowledge, may they have Your understanding; and above all opinions, may they have Your wisdom.

Nearness

Be their God in their going out and coming in, their life choices and decisions, their waiting times and busy times, their happy times and times of sorrow, their times of testing and times of celebration.

Meaning and Purpose

I believe we have been brought into this world for redemption rather than destruction, peace rather than panic, completeness rather than emptiness, and the glorification of Your name rather than frustration.

Freedom

May they live free of fear—safe from its bondage, kept from its paralyzing grip, protected from everything that would terrify them. Keep them free from anything that would hinder them as they seek to experience Your perfect plan for their lives.

Strength

May my children look to You, trust in You, and lean upon Your resources every moment of every day. When facing temptation, make them strong to resist. Give them the strength to say no to everything that would draw them away from You and yes to everything that will draw them closer to Your heart.

Victory

Help my children, by Your grace, to stand firm against every scheme of the devil, be strong, grow daily in their faith and confidence in You, and pray for others with a sincere heart of love and understanding.

Section Two

THE COMFORT OF PROTECTION

The Comfort of Protection

This I declare about the LORD: He alone is my refuge,
my place of safety; he is my God, and I trust him.
...He will cover you with His feathers. He will
shelter you with His wings. His faithful promises
are your armor and protection.
Psalm 91:2,4 NLT

It's important for children to feel safe and secure. Many things can cause them to become frightened and insecure—a dark room, a loud noise, unfamiliar surroundings, a strange face, a thunderstorm. The need to be sheltered, protected, and cared for remains with us throughout life.

When the disciples were with Jesus on a stormy sea, they became fearful and came to Him for help (He was asleep on the boat at the time). It took Jesus but a moment to quiet the storm and calm their fears. They needed reassurance that they were in the presence of the one who cared about them and could protect them from any storm.

Through prayer, you can ask that each day your children will be reassured of God's presence, His watch care, His hand of covering, and His ever-present help in every time of need.

This section's promises focus on the following needs:

Favor

Care

Abundance

Acceptance

Answered Prayer

Holiness

Favor

Promise

Behold, children are a heritage
*and gift from the L*ORD*,*
the fruit of the womb a reward.
Like arrows in the hand of a warrior,
so are the children of one's youth.
How blessed [happy and fortunate] is the man
whose quiver is filled with them;
they will not be ashamed when they speak
with their enemies [in gatherings] at the [city] gate.

Psalm 127:3–5 AMP

Prayer

Heavenly Father, my prayer today is one of thanksgiving, gratitude, and praise. Thank You for Your favor and marvelous generosity to me and my family. Every one of Your good and perfect gifts to us comes directly from Your hand by way of Your giving heart of kindness and love.

I cannot begin to express how greatly blessed and grateful I am for the gift of my children. With all my heart, I receive each life that has come into our family as Your beautiful gift. I cannot find the words to thank You enough.

My children are a testimony of Your grace, a proclamation of Your wisdom, a revelation of Your workmanship, and a demonstration of the creative work of Your hands. I thank You for giving them to us as Your heritage—to know, enjoy, love, care for, celebrate, delight in, and raise so that they may know You and receive Your Son as their greatest gift of all.

Care

Promise

You have taught children and infants
to tell of your strength,
silencing your enemies and all who oppose you.
When I look at the night sky
and see the work of your fingers—the moon
and the stars you set in place—what are mere mortals
that you should think about them,
human beings that you should care for them?

Psalm 8:2–4 NLT

Prayer

Lord God of the universe, Designer and Maker of all that is in the heavens and upon the earth, I thank You that You are mighty and You alone do marvelous things. I thank You that You made my children with Your own hands, You shaped them, You breathed into them the breath of life, and You also look out for each one. Reveal to them Your mighty strength, Your awesome power, and Your infinite wisdom.

I am amazed by Your greatness and how much You care about the lives of my children. You see, know, understand, and care about every detail of their lives. It is in You that they live, move, and have their being.

I'm so thankful that my children are on Your mind and in Your thoughts today. I pray that their hearts would trust in You and turn toward You, while their feet follow You all the days of their lives.

Abundance

Promise

Young men and young women,
old men and children.
Let them all praise the name of the LORD.
For his name is very great;
his glory towers over the earth and heaven!
He has made his people strong,
honoring his faithful ones—the people of Israel
who are close to him. Praise the LORD!

Psalm 148:12–14 NLT

Prayer

Father, may my children see You, hear You, and love You more each day. May they taste and see that You are good. May they touch You with the hand of faith and know the reality of Your presence. May their days be full of joy and each day of their lives be blessed.

I ask that with each passing day, they would realize to a greater degree—how great You are, how glorious are Your ways, and how awesome are Your works. May they sing Your songs of joy and speak Your words of life. May they sound forth Your praises and live with worship in their hearts. May truth fill their minds, wisdom fill their understanding, and their tongues bring forth constant gratitude and thankfulness.

Lord, keep my children strong in Your strength, blessed with Your blessings, and full with Your abundance as they see Your faithfulness revealed to them day by day.

Acceptance

Promise

*They brought little children to Him, that He might touch
them; but the disciples rebuked those who brought them.
But when Jesus saw it, He was greatly displeased and
said to them, "Let the little children come to Me,
and do not forbid them; for of such is the kingdom of
God. Assuredly, I say to you, whoever does not receive
the kingdom of God as a little child will by no means
enter it." And He took them up in His arms, laid
His hands on them, and blessed them.*

Mark 10:13–16 NKJV

Prayer

Jesus, I thank You for the wonderful privilege of knowing I can bring my children to You in prayer. It means so much to me to know that each child means so much to You.

Thank You for not pushing my children away from You or keeping them at a distance. Thank You for welcoming them with outstretched arms, embracing them with a full heart of compassion, receiving them fully, and drawing them close to You.

Today, Jesus, I ask You to place Your hand upon the heads of my children. I ask You to bless them with the richest blessings of Your hidden treasures. Touch their lives, warm their hearts, fill their cups, make them whole, and keep them strong. Teach them Your ways, and reveal to them the greatness of Your kingdom, the meekness of Your spirit, and the beauty of Your ways.

Answered Prayer

Promise

I asked the Lord to give me this boy,
and he has granted my request.
Now I am giving him to the Lord,
and he will belong to the Lord
his whole life.

1 Samuel 1:27–28 NKJV

Prayer

Heavenly Father, I thank You for Your full, generous, giving heart. I thank You for inviting, encouraging, and welcoming me to come to You in prayer, sit at Your banqueting table and dine with You, and enjoy the fullness of Your presence.

I thank You for allowing me to bring to You the prayers of my heart—carrying with them my deepest longings and strongest desires. I thank You for hearing my heart's cry and giving me, through my children, more than I could ask or dream. What a blessing and joy each answered prayer is to me. Each one helps me to see and understand Your heart more clearly.

Today, I affirm anew, that I fully give back to You the gift of the children You have so generously given me. I place them in Your hands and into Your keeping. Continue to give me the wisdom to guide each of their steps in Your pathway, and help each one to know Your plan and purpose for each phase of their lives.

Holiness

Promise

Call them all together—men, women, children,
and the foreigners living in your towns—so they may
hear this Book of Instruction and learn
to fear the LORD your God and carefully obey
all the terms of these instructions.
Do this so that your children who have not
known these instructions will hear them
and will learn to fear the LORD your God.

Deuteronomy 31:12–13 NLT

Prayer

Lord, You have said that to fear You with reverential awe is the beginning of wisdom and moves our lives away from evil. I pray that the fear of the Lord would be established deep within my heart and the hearts of each of my children.

I pray that we would daily stand in the light of Your holiness with broken and contrite hearts; bow before You with meek and quiet spirits; and kneel at Your feet in quiet worship as we behold Your glory and majesty. I pray that because we fear You, we will always run toward You. I pray that we would always understand that to fear You means we would never desire to do anything that grieves or saddens Your heart.

May we live to bring a smile to Your face. May we always care about what You think and how You feel. As You bless us, Lord, I pray that each one in our family will daily be a blessing to You.

At the Heart of the Prayer

A key focus of each prayer to carry in your heart.

Favor

I cannot begin to express how greatly blessed and grateful I am for the gift of my children. With all my heart, I receive each life that has come into our family as Your beautiful gift. I cannot find the words to thank You enough.

Care

I am amazed by Your greatness and how much You care about the lives of my children. You see, know, understand, and care about every detail of their lives. It is in You that they live, move, and have their being.

Abundance

Lord, keep my children strong in Your strength, blessed with Your blessings, and full with Your abundance as they see Your faithfulness revealed to them day by day.

Acceptance

Today, Jesus, I ask You to place Your hand upon my children's heads. I ask You to bless them with the richest blessings of Your hidden treasures. Touch their lives, warm their hearts, fill their cups, make them whole, and keep them strong.

Answered Prayer

I thank You for allowing me to bring to You the prayers of my heart—carrying with them my deepest longings and strongest desires. I thank You for hearing my heart's cry and giving me, through my children, more than I could ask or dream.

Holiness

I pray that because we fear You, we will always run toward You. I pray that we would always understand that to fear You means we would never desire to do anything that grieves or saddens Your heart.

Section Three

THE BEAUTY OF CHARACTER

The Beauty of Character

Let the beauty of the L𝗈𝗋𝖽 our God be upon us.
Psalm 90:17 KJV

Like clay, our lives need to be formed, molded, and shaped into the image of the God who created us. Godly character is not a gift that we instantly receive, but something that is formed within us by placing our lives in God's hands, receiving His grace, depending on His Spirit, and choosing to do what is pleasing in His sight.

It is important for parents to pray that their children will not only know the Lord and follow Him but also yield themselves to the Lord so that His character can be formed within them. No life is more beautiful than the one whose heart is filled with loveliness, whose attitudes are filled with kindness, whose words are spoken with gentleness, and whose behavior is marked by righteousness.

This section's promises focus on the following needs:

Guidance

Foundations

Character

Eternal Life

Celebration Instruction

Guidance

Promise

Direct your children onto the right path,
and when they are older,
they will not leave it.

Proverbs 22:6 NLT

Prayer

Father, I need to know Your direction in my life so that I can rightly bring direction to my children's lives. I need Your training so that I can train them up in the way they should go. I ask for daily wisdom to speak the right things and do the right things. Place Your words in my mouth and guide my footsteps in Your pathway. Give me Your wisdom so that I am able to give wise guidance, Your holy love so that I am able to choose what is truly best, Your light and understanding so that I am able to clearly point the way to Your will.

I thank You for Your promise to keep my children on the right path. I pray that they will love Your ways and Your will and carry Your songs of joy in their hearts. May their relationships with You be strong and growing.

I pray that my children will always walk in what is good, what is true, and what is right. May they celebrate the lives You have given them, appreciate their uniqueness, and fully embrace the desires You place within their hearts.

Foundations

Promise

Exult in his holy name;
rejoice, you who worship the Lᴏʀᴅ.
Search for the Lᴏʀᴅ and for his strength;
continually seek him. Remember the wonders
he has performed, his miracles,
and the rulings he has given.

Psalm 105:3–5 NLT

Prayer

Lord, as my children grow, I ask that they will never outgrow their pursuit of Your will, their desire for Your ways, their hunger for Your Word, their dependency on Your strength, and their need for Your grace. May the spiritual foundations established in their hearts when they are young help them as they grow to build strong lives of faith and obedience, hope and trust, righteousness and freedom, love and compassion.

May they remember everything You do for them, everything You have provided for them, everything You have taught them, and everything You have done to bless them.

Lord, bless them with good memories, keen understanding, sweet remembrances, sound minds, and practical understanding. May we all cherish, with full hearts, all Christ has done for us—for the blood He shed, the forgiveness He extended, the salvation He provided, and the love He has freely given.

Character

Promise

*I pray that your love will overflow more and more, and
that you will keep on growing in knowledge
and understanding.
For I want you to understand what really matters,
so that you may live pure and blameless lives
until the day of Christ's return.
May you always be filled with the fruit of your
salvation—the righteous character produced
in your life by Jesus Christ—for this will bring much
glory and praise to God.*

Philippians 1:9–11 NLT

Prayer

Father, bless my children and make them a blessing. May Christ be formed in them. As their Potter, shape and mold their character and use them where You place them. I know that everything You make is beautiful!

Help my children know how to follow You so they will be able to lead others. Help them know how to give freely so that they will prosper in the true riches of Your kingdom. Help them know how to yield to Your will so they will be able to stand strong in Your grace and sufficiency.

May my children be wise students, good workers, supportive team members, and loyal companions. Help them live productive and fruitful lives. Teach them to walk as You walked and honor their Father in heaven, just as You honored Him when You walked on the earth. May their days be long, their hearts be full, their lives be enriched, and their blessings be abundant.

Eternal Life

Promise

This is eternal life: that they may know You,
the only true [supreme and sovereign] God,
and [in the same manner know] Jesus [as the] Christ
whom You have sent.

John 17:3 AMP

Prayer

Today I want to thank You, Lord, for revealing Yourself to us so that we will not only know about You but each of us will know You personally. My heart is filled with gratitude when I realize that Your Word says we are known by You as well. I ask that all my children will come to know You in their hearts and lives, for there can be nothing higher or greater than that!

May all my children know You in Your holiness, Your beauty, and Your glory. May they know You in Your wonders and in Your ways; in Your power and in Your splendor; in Your might and in Your majesty. May they look to You as their Father, depend on You as their Friend, trust in You as their Provider, yield to You as their Lord, and serve You as their King.

Above all, may they always be assured that You know all about them. May they rest in the assurance of Your daily care. Thank You for the privilege we have of knowing You and being known by You.

Celebration

Promise

They said to Him, "Do You hear what these children are
saying?" And Jesus replied to them,
"Yes; have you never read [in the Scripture],
'OUT OF THE MOUTHS OF INFANTS AND NURSING BABIES
YOU HAVE PREPARED and PROVIDED PRAISE FOR YOURSELF'?"

Matthew 21:16 AMP

Prayer

Father in heaven, holy is Your name. I ask that my children will be Your true worshipers. I ask that they will worship You in spirit and in truth. I pray that they will see Your glory, be at Your feet, behold Your face, and be overcome by Your beauty. May Your praise daily be upon their lips. May they never lose the awe that comes from fixing their gaze on You.

May my children worship You with the music of praise, as well as words of gratitude, actions of love, attitudes of righteousness, shouts of joy, and new songs of the Spirit that are born out of a deep devotion to You.

I ask that their lives will be a daily celebration. May they continually drink from the river of Your mercies, break bread at Your table, and delight themselves in the pleasures of Your companionship. May they always walk in Your freshest footsteps, in newness of life, in fellowship with Your people, and in the joys of their salvation. And thank You for the joy You give as they continue to experience You in their lives.

Instruction

Promise

My child, listen when your father corrects you.
Don't neglect your mother's instruction.
What you learn from them will crown you with grace
and be a chain of honor around your neck.

Proverbs 1:8–9 NLT

Prayer

Thank You, Lord, for the place and privilege You have given me in the lives of my children. I am so grateful that You have ordained me, by Your grace and Holy Spirit, to speak into their lives through a right example—with wise words, loving correction, and practical instruction. I pray that my children will continue to grow in wisdom as they hear Your instruction, read Your Word, and learn from the circumstances and relationships You bring into their lives.

I pray that my children will always be good hearers of Your voice and strong followers of Your will. Help them see life from Your point of view and make choices with eternal values in mind.

I ask that they will learn to recognize Your voice, treasure Your truth, and seek Your approval. May they live each day with the crown of Your grace upon their heads and the chain of Your honor and favor around their necks.

At the Heart of the Prayer

A key focus of each prayer to carry in your heart.

Guidance

I pray that my children will love Your ways and Your will, and carry Your songs of joy in their hearts. May their relationships with You be strong and growing.

Foundations

I pray that the spiritual foundations established in their hearts when they are young will help them as they grow to build strong lives of faith and obedience, hope and trust, righteousness and freedom, love and compassion.

Character

Lord, teach them to walk as You walked and honor their Father in heaven, just as You honored Him when You walked on the earth. May their days be long, their hearts be full, their lives be enriched, and their blessings be abundant.

Eternal Life

May all of my children look to You as their Father, depend on You as their Friend, trust in You as their Provider, yield to You as their Lord, and serve You as their King.

Celebration

May my children worship You with the music of praise, as well as words of gratitude, actions of love, attitudes of righteousness, shouts of joy, and new songs of the Spirit that are born out of a deep devotion to You.

Instruction

I pray that my children will continue to grow in wisdom as they hear Your instruction, read Your Word, and learn from the circumstances and relationships You bring into their lives.

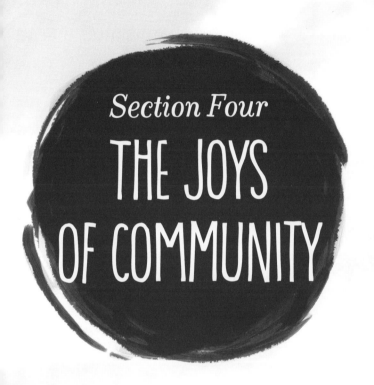

Section Four

THE JOYS OF COMMUNITY

The Joys of Community

Through love serve one another.
Colossians 5:13 NKJV

God has not only called us to know and enjoy Him but He has also called us to know and enjoy others. Each child of God has been placed into a family of believers. The outflow of our fellowship with God will bring us into fellowship with others. God has made us dependent upon one another. We need other people, and they need us to grow and be supported, helped, encouraged, loved, prayed for, enriched, guided, cared for, and blessed.

As children grow and mature, parents need to be in prayer about the friendships their children form and the influence their lives will have upon others. Through every stage of life children can be a blessing to those around them, including family members, classmates, teachers, and others in the community.

This section's promises focus on the following needs:

Truth in Relationshipse

Humility

The Kingdom of Godr

Remembrance

Revelation

Light of the Lord

Truth in Relationships

Promise

My child, if sinners entice you,

turn your back on them!...

My child, don't go along with them!

Stay far away from their paths.

Proverbs 1:10,15 NLT

Do not be deceived:

"Bad company corrupts good morals."

1 Corinthians 15:33 AMP

Prayer

Heavenly Father, thank You for the truth and light my children receive from Your Word. Thank You for Your wisdom that has the power to keep them from going through heartaches and sorrows You never intended for them to experience.

I pray that my children will learn to trust in Your Word to guide them in the decisions they make. I pray they will know beyond a doubt that Your ways are best. I pray that they will be assured that You will not withhold any good thing from them and have the peace and satisfaction of knowing that their obedience to You means living without regrets.

I also ask You to bless my children in their relationships throughout their lives. May they know what it means to be a good friend, and may they always be blessed with good friends—those who are growing in faith, strong in character, upright in conduct, loyal and supportive, true and trusting, helpful and kind-of-heart.

Humility

Promise

You younger men, likewise, be subject to your elders;
and all of you, clothe yourselves with humility
toward one another, for GOD IS OPPOSED TO THE PROUD,
BUT GIVES GRACE TO THE HUMBLE.
Therefore humble yourselves under the mighty hand
of God, that He may exalt you at the proper time.

I Peter 5:5–6 NASB

Prayer

God, I thank You for being my all-in-all, for being above all, and ruling over all that is in heaven and on earth. Thank You for those You place over my children, and thank You for using those individuals to help shape them, mold their character, conform them to Your image, and prepare them for the things You have planned for them.

I pray that my children will be honoring to those You have placed over them. I pray they will give honor to everyone, especially the elderly, and learn to know Your heart when You said, "I have not come to be served but to serve."

I pray that my children's hearts will never be filled with pride, puffed up, or prone to look down on others. May they be humble vessels who are aware of their needs, who are broken and contrite before You, and who realize, moment by moment, their total dependency upon Your grace.

The Kingdom of God

Promise

Just as it is written [in Scripture], "THINGS WHICH THE EYE HAS NOT SEEN AND THE EAR HAS NOT HEARD, AND WHICH HAVE NOT ENTERED THE HEART OF MAN, ALL THAT GOD HAS PREPARED FOR THOSE WHO LOVE HIM [who hold Him in affectionate reverence, who obey Him, and who gratefully recognize the benefits that He has bestowed]."
For God has unveiled them and revealed them to us through the [Holy] Spirit; for the Spirit searches all things [diligently], even [sounding and measuring] the [profound] depths of God [the divine counsels and things far beyond human understanding].

I Corinthians 2:9–10 AMP

Prayer

Heavenly Father, thank You for the realities of Your kingdom, and thank You for preparing more for us to see, hear, and know in our hearts than we could have ever imagined. I pray that the realities of Your unseen world will always have a greater influence on the lives of my children than the realities of the physical world they see, hear, and touch each day.

May my children see You with spiritual eyes, hear You with spiritual ears, and touch You with the outstretched hand of faith. May Your light fill their vision, Your touch warm their hearts, and Your voice be the loudest sound they hear within them.

Father, I ask that Your Holy Spirit will continue to show my children things their eyes have never seen, speak things their ears have never heard, and reveal things their hearts have never known about the wonders You have prepared for them.

Remembrance

Promise

Can a woman forget her nursing child,
and not have compassion on the son of her womb?
Surely they may forget, yet I will not forget you.
See, I have inscribed you on the palms of My hands;
your walls are continually before Me.

Isaiah 49:15–16 NKJV

Prayer

Thank You, Father, for being a God of compassion who feels deeply and cares greatly for my family. Thank You that through Your compassion, my children can know Your inner feelings for each of them personally, sense Your tender touch upon them, see the riches of what Your heart holds for them, and experience the fullness of what Your love brings to them.

Father, I am amazed to realize that Your love for my children is even greater than the love I have for them and that the depth of Your feelings for them goes even deeper than what I hold for them. What a great comfort it is to know how much You care for them, and that they are always in Your thoughts.

May my children always be aware of how much they mean to You, how precious they are in Your sight, how tenderly You carry them in Your thoughts, and that their names are written on the palms of Your compassionate hands.

Revelation

Promise

*The secret things belong to the L*ORD *our God,*
but the things which are revealed and disclosed
belong to us and to our children forever,
so that we may do all of the words of this law.

Deuteronomy 29:29 AMP

Prayer

Lord, how wonderful are Your ways, how great is Your understanding, how vast is Your knowledge, how deep is Your love, how wise are Your plans, how mighty is Your strength, how complete is Your salvation, and how perfect is Your Word. Thank You for revealing to my children all they need to know in order to find Your purpose and fulfill Your will for their lives.

I pray that my children will be seekers of Your treasures, finders of Your blessings, receivers of Your gifts, discoverers of the riches found in Your grace, possessors of Your abundant life, and explorers who discover the hidden wealth that is found upon Your pathways.

Open up to them, Lord, the knowledge that will guide their understanding and the wisdom that will direct their footsteps. Assure them that they will always have enough light to take the next step and do the next thing. I pray that they will receive and experience all that belongs to them in Christ. May their greatest delight be found in the joys of their obedience to You.

Light of the Lord

Promise

How precious is Your lovingkindness, O God!
The children of men take refuge in the shadow of
Your wings. They drink their fill of the abundance of
Your house; and You allow them to drink from the river
of Your delights. For with You is the fountain of life [the
fountain of life-giving water]; in Your light we see light.

Psalm 36:7–9 AMP

Prayer

I thank You, Lord, that You are Light and in You there is no darkness, no shadow, no confusion, no lying, and no deceit. Thank You for being the Light of the World and the Light of Life. Thank You for Your assurance that Your light never flickers, grows dim, burns out, or goes out.

I pray that my children will see the splendor of Your light—that its beam will shine upon their pathway, its flame warm their hearts, its beauty lift their spirits, and its glow shine upon their faces. Send Your light, Lord, to inspire my children, build their faith, renew their hope, strengthen their courage, lighten their steps, and encourage them on their spiritual journey.

Give my children clear direction for the future, straight paths for their feet, and enough light to take the next step. Lead them in the way everlasting.

At the Heart of the Prayer

A key focus of each prayer to carry in your heart.

Truth in Relationships

I also ask that you will bless my children in their relationships throughout their lives. May they know what it means to be a good friend, and may they always be blessed with good friends—those who are growing in faith, strong in character, upright in conduct, loyal and supportive, true and trusting, helpful and kind-of-heart.

Humility

I pray that my children will be honoring to those You have placed over them. I pray they will give honor to everyone, especially the elderly, and learn to know Your heart when You said, "I have not come to be served but to serve."

The Kingdom of God

I pray that the realities of Your unseen world will always have a greater influence on the lives of my children than the realities of the physical world they see, hear, and touch each day.

Remembrance

May my children always be aware of how much they mean to You, how precious they are in Your sight, how tenderly You carry them in Your thoughts, and that their names are written on the palms of Your compassionate hands.

Revelation

I pray that my children will be seekers of Your treasures, finders of Your blessings, receivers of Your gifts, discoverers of the riches found in Your grace, possessors of Your abundant life, and explorers who discover the hidden wealth that is found upon Your pathways.

Light of the Lord

Give my children clear direction for the future, straight paths for their feet, and enough light to take the next step. Lead them in the way everlasting.

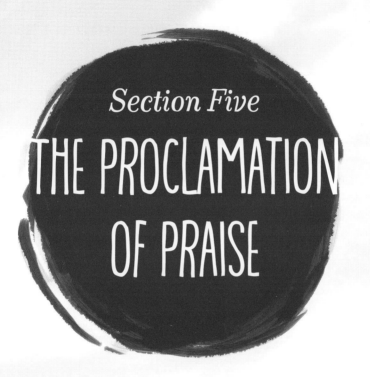

Section Five

THE PROCLAMATION OF PRAISE

The Proclamation of Praise

Let everything that has breath praise the LORD.
Praise the LORD.
Psalm 150:6 NKJV

We were made to celebrate, be filled with gladness, and have our hearts overflow with joy. Praise should always be on our lips and thanksgiving in our hearts. We were made to have God at the center of our joy and as the focus of our praise. It is from Him, to Him, and through Him that our voices can rejoice evermore, our mouths can be filled with laughter, and our hearts can find, at His right hand, the pleasures that are ours forevermore.

Pray that your children will have happy dispositions, live contented lives, and sing new songs unto the Lord. Pray that their cups will be full and running over, that they will be worshipers of God in spirit and truth, and that they will always carry a melody of praise in their hearts.

This section's promises focus on the following needs:

Prosperity

Fulfilled Promises

Growth

Daily Bread

Courage

Overwhelming

Prosperity

Promise

I know the thoughts that I think toward you,
*says the L*ORD*, thoughts of peace and not of evil,*
to give you a future and a hope.

Jeremiah 29:11 NKJV

Prayer

Lord, I'm thankful that You know all things and can be fully trusted because You are completely faithful. Thank You for the wisdom of Your ways and the goodness of Your plans. I know You have only good things in Your heart for my children. Thank You for Your assurance that they will never have to guess or find their own way in life because You will lead and guide them in the way they should go.

I thank You that my children's future is bright because Your light shines upon them, their future is right because You have planned it, and their future is victorious because Your might has secured it. I ask You, Lord, to prosper each of my children—make each one rich in Your riches, strong in Your strength, and blessed with Your blessings.

I ask that Your perfect plan for each one be accomplished as they yield their hearts to You, put their trust in You, and follow Your pathways. Thank You for being their certain hope and glorious future.

Fulfilled Promises

Promise

*The promise [of the Holy Spirit] is for you and your
children and for all who are far away
[including the Gentiles], as many as the Lord our God
calls to Himself.*

Acts 2:39 AMP

Prayer

Thank You, God, my Promise Maker and Promise Keeper. Thank You for giving me promises to trust in and fulfill in Your perfect time. I'm thankful that Your timing is never too late, You never make an empty promise, You never forget a promise You have made, and You never make a mistake.

I thank You, God, that Your promises are not just for generations past but also for my generation and my children's generation. Thank You that what You promised the early church, You have also promised us. May my children's hearts always rest assured that You are not only the promise keeper of the past but also the promise keeper of today and the promise keeper of their futures.

Thank You that Your promises to my children are the divine assurances of Your will. I ask that You fulfill in them the promise of the fullness of Your Holy Spirit, the promise of Your call upon their lives, and the promise of Your presence with them always.

Growth

Promise

The Child continued to grow and become strong
[in spirit], filled with wisdom; and the grace
(favor, spiritual blessing) of God was upon Him.

Luke 2:40 AMP

Prayer

Lord Jesus, thank You for coming to this earth, taking on human flesh, living among us, and doing Your Father's will. Thank You for the way You lived and what You taught us through Your words and Your life.

I pray that my children will grow in the same ways You grew. May they have a sharp focus and clear purpose; may they know why they are here and where they are going; may they have the inner strength to grow strong in character; and may they always be about their heavenly Father's business. I pray that my children will grow, not only in years but also in depth of love and maturity. Give them wholeness in body, soul, and spirit. Bless them with good health, and may their desires be set on doing all that is pleasing to You. May they be filled with wisdom and may Your grace, favor, and spiritual blessings be upon them.

Above all, I ask that my children will be strong in spirit— being at Your feet, knowing Your worthiness, intimate in their relationships with You, supping at Your table, and communing with You daily.

Daily Bread

Promise

Your words were found, and I ate them,
and Your word was to me the joy and rejoicing
of my heart; for I am called by Your name,
*O L*ord *God of hosts.*

Jeremiah 15:16 NKJV

Prayer

Gracious Father, thank You that my children can know Your heart and hear Your heart through the words You have spoken. I'm thankful that Your words are like no other—their taste is sweet, their sound is a symphony, and their power is a transforming light. They are a lamp to my children's feet and a light to their pathway. I ask that they will always hunger after Your words. Increase their appetite. May they find Your words to be delightful, whole, and pure, abundant in grace, and rich in mercy. Feed them, Father, with fresh bread, living bread, and daily bread.

Nurture them in their spirits. Teach them that they cannot live on bread alone; they need You to sustain them with every word that comes from Your mouth. Break to them the bread of life.

I thank You, Father, that Your words can be found, Your words can be eaten, and Your words can be known. May my children find Your words to be the joy and rejoicing of their hearts. Each day, may they realize the awesome privilege they have to be called by Your name, receive Your words, and be a part of Your forever family.

Courage

Promise

"Be strong and of good courage,
do not fear nor be afraid of them;
for the LORD your God, He is the One
who goes with you.
He will not leave you nor forsake you..."
And the LORD, He is the one who goes before you.
He will be with you, He will not leave you
nor forsake you; do not fear nor be dismayed."

Deuteronomy 31:6,8 NKJV

Prayer

I thank You, Lord, that You are the mighty God—all powerful and without limitation—and there are no impossibilities to what You can do. I pray that my children will find their strength in Your strength, and that they may live victorious lives because You have gone before them and conquered every foe.

May my children's hands be joined in Yours, touching as You touch; may their feet follow Your footsteps, moving as You move; may their hearts be one with Yours, feeling as You feel; may their wills be one with Your will, working as You work.

I ask that each of my children will be strong, all of them walking with You. May their courage be unwavering, their obedience complete, and their purpose certain. Lord, assure them that they will never need to walk in fear or doubt. They can be courageous because You go with them. You will not fail them, nor will You forsake them.

Overcoming

Promise

You are of God, little children,
and have overcome them,
because He who is in you is greater
than he who is in the world.

I John 4:4 NKJV

Prayer

Thank You, Jesus, for Your life, Your death, and Your resurrection. They have transformed my life, and they are able to transform the lives of my children. Thank You also for facing Satan and defeating him, living in the world and overcoming it, facing temptation and refusing to yield to it, and tasting death and defeating it.

I pray that my children and I will see You in Your glory, know You in Your fullness, and live our lives in Your overcoming power. May we know You, not just as Savior, Friend, and Shepherd but also as our very life. I thank You, Jesus, that Your life in my children is greater than anything they will face in this world because You have overcome the world. Make them overcomers as well. May they always respond in quick obedience to You.

Keep my children from temptation, protect them from the evil one, and establish their hearts in Your truth. May they always know that because You live in them, they can live abundantly, purposefully, and victoriously.

At the Heart of the Prayer

A key focus of each prayer to carry in your heart.

Prosperity

I ask You, Lord, to prosper each of my children—make each one rich in Your riches, strong in Your strength, and blessed with Your blessings.

Fulfilled Promises

May my children's hearts always rest assured that You are not only the promise keeper of the past but also the promise keeper of today and the promise keeper of their futures.

Growth

I pray that my children will grow, not only in years but also in depth of love and maturity. Give them wholeness in body, soul, and spirit. Bless them with good health, and may their desires be set on doing all that is pleasing to You.

Daily Bread

May my children find Your words to be delightful, whole, and pure, abundant in grace, and rich in mercy. Feed them, Father, with fresh bread, living bread, and daily bread.

Courage

I ask that each of my children will be strong, all of them walking with You. May their courage be unwavering, their obedience complete, and their purpose certain.

Overcoming

I thank You, Jesus, that Your life in my children is greater than anything they will face in this world because You have overcome the world. Make them overcomers as well. May they always respond in quick obedience to You.

Section Six

THE BENEFITS OF GROWTH

The Benefits of Growth

Grow in the grace and knowledge of our Lord and Savior Jesus Christ. To Him be the glory both now and forever.
2 Peter 3:18 NKJV

A newborn baby brings a special joy and delight far beyond what words can express. Loving parents seek to train, teach, help, and pray for their children, trusting that their little ones will grow up to have responsible and productive lives, while faithfully fulfilling the unique plan God has for each of them.

Through prayer, parents can ask God to plant the eternal seed of His life within the hearts of their children. They can pray that this seed will be watered by His Word and warmed by the sunshine of His presence, love, and care. Prayer can also cover that seed and protect it until it has become rooted in love, full-grown in grace, and a fruitful and flourishing vine within their children's lives.

This section's promises focus on the following needs:

Completion

Reality

The Kingdom of Godr

Remembrance

Revelation

Light of the Lord

Completion

Promise

I am convinced and confident of this very thing,
that He who has begun a good work in you will
[continue to] perfect and complete it until the day of
Christ Jesus [the time of His return].

Philippians 1:6 AMP

Prayer

Thank You, Father, that You are a faithful God in whom I can put my complete trust. I am so grateful for the way You are working in my life and in the lives of my children. I thank You that the work You are doing is a beautiful work, a good work, and a perfect work—full of promise and hope. Thank You, that You do not begin a work within us and then leave it up to us to complete.

I ask that my children's trust and faith in You will continue to grow. May they be confident, convinced, and fully persuaded in their hearts that You will never fail them. May they be assured that the work You have begun in them will continue and come to completion.

Thank You that by Your Holy Spirit, You are making my children into all You desire them to be. Father, breathe Your life into them and form Your image within them until You have accomplished what is pleasing to You.

Reality

Promise

Of Him you are in Christ Jesus, who became for
us wisdom from God—and righteousness and
sanctification and redemption—that, as it is written,
"He who glories, let him glory in the LORD."

I Corinthians 1:30–31 NKJV

Prayer

Heavenly Father, thank You for Jesus, Your only begotten Son, Your perfect gift, the One who is too wonderful for words! Thank You that Jesus not only lives at Your right hand in heaven but also within the hearts of those who believe in and receive Him.

Thank You for making it possible for my children to know Jesus—personally, truly, intimately, and completely. I ask that they never know a fake or pretend life but only the real life You have made possible for them. May their hearts fully understand what it means to believe in Jesus and also to be in Jesus.

May my children know in reality that Jesus is their life—their wisdom, righteousness, holiness, purity, goodness, redemption, hope, and future. May they all live a life of joyful celebration over their relationships with Jesus. May they be caught up in His beauty, filled up with His love, and fully committed to making Him known to this generation.

Spiritual Blessings

Promise

Grace to you and peace from God
our Father and the Lord Jesus Christ.
Blessed be the God and Father of our Lord Jesus Christ,
who has blessed us with every spiritual blessing
in the heavenly places in Christ,
just as He chose us in Him
before the foundation of the world,
that we should be holy and without blame
before Him in love.

Ephesians 1:2–4 NKJV

Prayer

Father, how gracious You are, how blessed I am, how rich is my portion, and how full is my cup! You are the perfect Father—loving, caring, providing, giving, sheltering—making a safe place, a restful place, a thriving place for me and my children to come to and abide in. Thank You that the best place, the highest place, and the most secure place for us to be is in Jesus Christ.

I pray that my children will be blessed with every spiritual blessing You have made available to them through their relationships with Your Son. May Your life be in them, Your hand be on them, and Your favor be over them. Work in them and through them.

Give all of us quiet hearts that trust in You, humble hearts that depend upon You, grateful hearts that receive from You, joyful hearts that worship You, true hearts that honor You, giving hearts that express You, pure hearts that glorify You, and faithful hearts that please You.

Encouragement

Promise

*Since we are surrounded by such a huge crowd
of witnesses to the life of faith,
let us strip off every weight that slows us down,
especially the sin that so easily trips us up.
And let us run with endurance the race God
has set before us.*

Hebrews 12:1 NLT

Prayer

Thank You, Lord, for the example provided by the men and women of faith whose lives are recounted in Your Word. Thank You for the testimonies of their trust, the fruits of their faithfulness, and the witness of their walk.

I pray that these faithful men and women will be a source of inspiration to my children. I pray also that the patience and endurance they exhibited will encourage my children to wait upon You in full confidence of faith. I ask that my children would be blessed with the blessings of Abraham!

May my children learn from Daniel, to be uncompromising; from Joseph, to do what is right by not sinning against You; from Gideon, to be strong and courageous; from Moses, to hear Your voice and see You do great and mighty things; from Ruth, to fully identify with You and Your people; from Sarah, to believe that You can do the impossible; from Samuel, to recognize Your voice and speak out Your words; and from David, to be a person after Your own heart.

Certainty

Promise

The Son of God, Jesus Christ, who was preached among you by us ... was not "Yes" and "No," but has proved to be "Yes" in Him [true and faithful, the divine "Yes" affirming God's promises]. For as many as are the promises of God, in Christ they are [all answered] "Yes." So through Him we say our "Amen" to the glory of God.

2 Corinthians 1:19–20 AMP

Prayer

Father, thank You that what is written in Your Word has been spoken from Your heart. I am grateful that Your promises come from the mouth of One who cannot lie. Not only have You given me and my family precious promises but You have guaranteed their fulfillment through Your Son, Jesus Christ.

I know that because Jesus is the Truth, Your promises are the truth. Because of Jesus, they are not meaningless, hollow words, but full of life, full of hope, and full of power. I ask that my children will keep their trust securely grounded in Your promises—no matter what!

When my children are in need, may they receive the promise of Your provision; when they are aware of their weaknesses, may they discover the promise of Your strength; when they are troubled, may they know the promise of Your peace; when they are seeking, may they find the promise of Your guidance; and when they recognize their inadequacy, may they embrace the promise of Your grace.

Provision

Promise

My God will liberally supply (fill until full)
your every need according to
His riches in glory in Christ Jesus.
To our God and Father be the glory forever and ever.
Amen.

Philippians 4:19–20 AMP

Prayer

Jesus, You are so wonderful! You are the One the Father has sent for us. May our hearts be taken up with You. May You be our daily song, our constant peace, our abundant joy, and our reason to live.

I ask that my children will always know how great and abundant is Your supply. I thank You that they can be lavished with the riches of Your grace. May they always be quick to come to You, trust in You, and receive from You.

Jesus, assure my children that they will never meet a fear You have not conquered, face an enemy You have not defeated, have a need You cannot meet, face a temptation You have not overcome, have a burden You cannot lift, face a problem You have not solved, struggle with a bondage You cannot break, or experience a moment when You do not care.

At the Heart of the Prayer

A key focus of each prayer to carry in your heart.

Completion

I ask that my children's trust and faith in You will continue to grow. May they be confident, convinced, and fully persuaded that You will never fail them. May they be assured that the work You have begun in them will continue and come to completion.

Reality

Thank You for making it possible for my children to know Jesus—personally, truly, intimately, and completely. I ask that my children never know a fake or pretend life but only the real life You have made possible for them.

Spiritual Blessings

I pray that my children will be blessed with every spiritual blessing that You have made available to them through their relationships with Your Son. May Your life be in them, Your hand be on them, and Your favor be over them. Work in them and through them.

Encouragement

Thank You, Lord, for the example provided by the men and women of faith whose lives are recounted in Your Word. Thank You for the testimonies of their trust, the fruits of their faithfulness, and the witness of their walk.

Certainty

Because of Jesus, Your promises are not meaningless, hollow words, but full of life, full of hope, and full of power. I ask that my children will keep their trust securely grounded in Your promises—no matter what!

Provision

Jesus, assure my children that they will never meet a fear You have not conquered, face an enemy You have not defeated, or have a need You cannot meet.

Section Seven

THE IMPACT OF COURAGE

The Impact of Courage

Be strong and let your heart take courage, all you who
wait for and hope for and expect the Lord!
Psalm 31:24 AMP

Courage impacts our lives and the lives of our children in powerful ways. Courage helps us move forward when we would rather turn back, face a problem when we would rather avoid it, resolve a difficulty when we would rather ignore it, do the right thing when the opportunity is there to compromise, and overcome rather than retreat or surrender.

A child, when alone, may lack the courage to walk on a pathway that leads through a dark and mysterious forest. However, when the child takes the hand of his father and walks with him on that pathway, courage comes. All the courage your children need to face life and its difficulties can be found in the Lord. Pray that they will be certain of His presence with them and confident that His provision will not fail. Pray that your children will live their lives with the assurance that God is all they need.

This section's promises focus on the following needs:

Endurance

Contentment

Focus

Protection

Worship

Peace

Endurance

Promise

We can rejoice, too, when we run into problems
and trials, for we know that they help us develop
endurance. And endurance develops
strength of character, and character strengthens
our confident hope of salvation.
And this hope will not lead to disappointment.
For we know how dearly God loves us.

Romans 5:3–5 NLT

Prayer

Father, I ask You to keep the hearts of my children close to You, their thoughts fixed on You, and their spirits strong in You. May Your grace draw them to Your heart, Your will, and Your love—moment by moment, day after day.

Help them to lean on You and draw their strength from You. Give them the endurance they need to stand firm, continue on, press in, and push through anything and everything that would hinder or sidetrack them from following Your plan and doing Your will. May we always have keen vision to watch out and correctly identify attacks from the devil—the vision to resist his temptations, reject his lies, refuse his condemnation, and debunk his accusations.

I pray that when my children are carrying burdens, they would cast them upon You; when they are anxious, they would depend upon Your promises; and when they become discouraged, their hope in You would be renewed. Assure them today, Father, how dearly You love them.

Contentment

Promise

Let your conduct be without covetousness;

be content with such things as you have.

For He Himself has said, "I will never leave you nor

forsake you." So we may boldly say:

"The Lᴏʀᴅ is my helper; I will not fear.

What can man do to me?"

Hebrews 13:5–6 NKJV

Prayer

I thank You, Gracious Father, for the wonderful ways You take care of my family. Thank You for the peace I have in knowing that even though our circumstances change, You never change. You are never inconsistent, undecided, unsure about what You should do, or limited in what You can do—Your resources cannot and will not ever be depleted.

I pray that my children will always live with contentment in their hearts—when they have much and when they have little. May they always enjoy an attitude of gratefulness, and may thanksgiving always be on their lips.

Father, give my children their daily bread. Bless them with simple pleasures, rich relationships, heartfelt joys, sufficient strength for their days, and the abundant fruit of their labors. Assure them in a thousand ways that You are their helper, and they need not fear.

Focus

Promise

[Looking away from all that will distract us and]
focusing our eyes on Jesus, who is the Author and
Perfecter of faith [the first incentive for our belief and the
One who brings our faith to maturity], who for the joy
[of accomplishing the goal] set before Him endured the
cross, disregarding the shame, and sat down at the right
hand of the throne of God [revealing His deity,
His authority, and the completion of His work].

Hebrews 12:2 AMP

Prayer

I thank You, Jesus, that it is all about You—Your work, Your ways, Your glory, Your life, and Your love. As I bring my children before You today, my prayer is that they will always—at all times, and in every situation—experience You at the very center of who they are and what they do.

May they see You as the one who came for them, died for them, rose for them, ascended for them, and lives for them. May they see You as their high priest who intercedes for them, their shepherd who guides them, their friend who cares about them, their counselor who speaks to them, and the great King of Kings who reigns over them.

May You always have the highest place—in their plans, in their choices, in their relationships, and in their desires. May Your smile greet them each morning; may Your song be within them each day; and may Your hand of tender mercies tuck them into bed each night.

Protection

Promise

You, O Lᴏʀᴅ, are a shield for me,
My glory [and my honor],
and the One who lifts my head.
With my voice I was crying to the Lᴏʀᴅ,
and He answered me from His holy mountain.
Selah.
I lay down and slept [safely];
I awakened, for the Lᴏʀᴅ sustains me.

Psalm 3:3–5 AMP

Prayer

Thank You, Lord, for being our hiding place, our safe place, and our shielded place. Thank You for being the defender and the protector of my children. I thank You for their safety today, knowing that the ministry of Your protective angels will be around them.

I ask for Your encouragement to be with them, Your hope to be in them, and Your grace to be upon them. If they are burdened, lighten their load; if they are troubled, calm their storm; if they are discouraged, lift their spirits; if they are unsure, strengthen their faith; if they are weary, renew their strength; if they are perplexed, guide their way; if they are unsteady, be their rock; if they are tempted, make a way of escape; if they lack understanding, be their wisdom; and if they doubt Your love, reveal Your heart.

Thank You for allowing me to call upon You knowing, with all certainty, that You hear my words, know my heart, and answer my prayers.

Worship

Promise

The sea is his, and he made it:
and his hands formed the dry land.
O come, let us worship and bow down:
*let us kneel before the L*ORD *our maker.*
For he is our God; and we are the people
of his pasture, and the sheep of his hand.

Psalm 95:5–7 KJV

Prayer

Lord, You are wonderful, and all that You do is marvelous in my sight. You are beyond description, and Your ways are past finding out. Your riches never tarnish, Your glory never grows dim, Your wonders never cease, Your beauty never fades, Your power never weakens, and Your love never ends. Thank You for being our God and allowing us to be Your people. Thank You for the beauty of the relationships we can have with You.

I pray that my children will worship You, both in spirit and in truth. May their hearts be caught up in Your majesty and their meditation be sweet. Each day, may they discover something new about the breadth, length, height, and depth of Your boundless, ceaseless love.

May my children's spirits find a resting place at Your altar; may their knees bend before You in true devotion; may their souls find the pleasures that await us at Your right hand; and may their hearts discover what it means to have fullness of joy.

Peace

Promise

May the God of peace who brought up
our Lord Jesus from the dead,
that great Shepherd of the sheep,
through the blood of the everlasting covenant,
make you complete in every good work to do His will,
working in you what is well pleasing in His sight,
through Jesus Christ,
to whom be glory forever and ever.
Amen.

Hebrews 13:20–21 NKJV

Prayer

Lord, my heart today joins in agreement with the prayer that is written in Hebrews 13:20–21. I ask that it will be specifically answered in the lives of my children. I pray that the perfect peace that only comes from You will guard each heart and mind. I thank You that Jesus is their shepherd and they are Your sheep. I thank You for feeding them when they are hungry, restoring them if they wander, and defending them when they are under attack. Thank You for being their door into Your green pastures.

I thank You, Lord, for Your shed blood and Your covenant promises. Thank You for all that Your shed blood has provided and purchased. Thank You that my children can overcome the enemy through the blood of the Lamb, and Your blood cleanses them from all sin.

Work Your will within my children. Bless them today through Jesus Christ. To You, Lord, be all the glory forever and ever. Amen.

At the Heart of the Prayer

A key focus of each prayer to carry in your heart.

Endurance

Father, I ask You to keep the hearts of my children close to You, keep their thoughts fixed on You, and keep their spirits strong in You. May Your grace draw them to Your heart, Your will, and Your love—moment by moment, day after day.

Contentment

Father, give my children their daily bread. Bless them with simple pleasures, rich relationships, heartfelt joys, sufficient strength for their days, and the fruit of their labors.

Focus

As I bring my children before You today, my prayer is that they will always—at all times, and in every situation—experience You at the very center of who they are and what they do.

Protection

Thank You, Lord, for being our hiding place, our safe place, and our shielded place. Thank You for being the defender and the protector of my children. I pray for their safety today, knowing that the ministry of Your protective angels will be around them.

Worship

I pray that my children will worship You, both in spirit and in truth. May their hearts be caught up in Your majesty and their meditation be sweet. Each day, may they discover something new about the breadth, length, height, and depth of Your boundless, ceaseless love.

Peace

Lord, my heart today joins in agreement with the prayer that is written in Hebrews 13:20–21. I ask that it will be specifically answered in the lives of my children. I pray that the perfect peace that only comes from You will guard each heart and mind.

Section Eight

THE POWER OF PURPOSE

The Power of Purpose

Never let loyalty and kindness leave you! Tie them around your neck as a reminder. Write them deep within your heart. Then you will find favor with both God and people, and you will earn a good reputation. Trust in the LORD with all your heart; do not depend on your own understanding. Seek His will in all you do, and He will show you which path to take.
Proverbs 3:3–6 NLT

There is great power in the life of someone who has a God-given purpose to fulfill, whose heart is passionate about that purpose, and whose will is set on fulfilling it. The plans of God for our lives should excite us, motivate us, and energize us to seek Him with all our being. His plans are only good, only right, only pure, and only the best.

Children need guidance and direction. They need to understand why they are here, where they are going, and how they will get there. They need to know that their lives have a God-given purpose waiting to be fulfilled. Parents need to pray that their children will know the plan God has for them, the path they are to follow, the steps they need to take, the direction they need to go, the dangers they need to avoid, the pace they need to travel, and the final destination of their journey.

This section's promises focus on the following needs:

Sufficiency

Fruitfulness

Fullness

Access

Kingdom Power

Unity

Sufficiency

Promise

I will exalt You, my God, O King,
and [with gratitude and submissive wonder]
I will bless Your name forever and ever.
Every day I will bless You and lovingly praise You;
yes, [with awe-inspired reverence],
I will praise Your name forever and ever.
Great is the LORD, and highly to be praised,
and His greatness is [so vast and profound as to be]
unsearchable [incomprehensible to man].

Psalm 145:1–3 AMP

Prayer

Lord, You are great! I pray that the eyes of my children will remain wide open to see Your awesomeness. May they know how vast is Your greatness, how deep is Your love, how high are Your ways, how rich are Your treasures, how abundant are Your blessings, how full are Your joys, and how generous are Your gifts.

May my children never think that You are too small, Your presence too distant, Your power too limited, Your love too conditional, Your help unavailable, or Your grace insufficient. In their inadequacies and human limitations may they learn to say, "I can do all things—big things, little things, unpleasant things, hard things, inconvenient things—through Christ who strengthens me."

Lord, I'm grateful that no matter how well my children know You, there is so much more to learn; no matter how much You have given them, there is so much more to receive; and no matter how much You have shown them, there is so much more to see.

Fruitfulness

Promise

*Blessed is the man who walks not in the counsel
of the ungodly... his delight is in the law of the L*ORD*,
and in His law he meditates day and night.
He shall be like a tree planted by the rivers of water,
that brings forth its fruit in its season,
whose leaf also shall not wither;
and whatever he does shall prosper.*

Psalm 1:1–3 NKJV

Prayer

Thank You, Lord, for the blessings that are ours as we walk in the way You counsel us, the way You lead us, and the way You have prepared for us. I pray that my children's values will be based on what You value, and Your approval will be their greatest delight.

I pray that my children will heed what You say in Your Word and mediate on Your instruction. I pray they will listen to what You are saying in their hearts and what they've received from You will be reflected through their behavior. May their lives be blessed like the tree that is planted by rivers of water. May their roots go down deep into Your wisdom, their branches blossom with Your understanding, and their lives bring forth the peaceful fruits of righteousness.

I pray that the lives of my children will grow strong, grow straight, and grow tall. I thank You for Your promise to nurture and prune them with the hands of a loving vinedresser so that the fruitfulness of their lives will increase and be abundant.

Fullness

Promise

I am the door. If anyone enters by Me,
he will be saved, and will go in and out
and find pasture...I have come that they may have life,
and that they may have it more abundantly.
I am the good shepherd.
The good shepherd gives His life for the sheep.

John 10:9–11 NKJV

Prayer

Lord Jesus, thank You for the door You have opened so that my family and I can enter into the life that is found in You.

Thank You for giving Your all so that we can have Your fullness, shedding Your blood so we can know Your forgiveness, and sending Your Holy Spirit so we can enjoy Your nearness. Thank You for teaching us what it means to be saved and know You, what it means to be cared for by You, and what it means to partake abundantly of the life that comes from You.

As I pray for my children today, I ask that they will come to know the height, breadth, length, and depth of Your abundant life. May they find the fulfillment of the deepest desires of their hearts—understanding why they are here and who You made them to be. May they find You to be the answer to every need of life—their need for love, acceptance, purpose, and meaning. May they hear Your voice calling them to Your heart.

Access

Promise

Open the gates to all who are righteous;
allow the faithful to enter.
You will keep in perfect peace all who trust in You,
all whose thoughts are fixed on You!
Trust in the LORD always,
for the LORD GOD is the eternal Rock.

Isaiah 26:2–4 NLT

Prayer

I am so thankful today, Father, for the open gates of access into Your presence and the open arms of access into Your love. There is no end to the riches we find in You. You are perfect in every way—without flaw, without error, without stain, without inconsistency, without hypocrisy, without deception, and without lies. I can safely put my complete trust in You.

I ask You to keep my children in perfect peace—the peace that only You can give, the peace that passes all understanding, the peace that knows "all is well" because You do all things well, the peace that proclaims with all certainty "You are in control," the peace that spreads its wings like the eagle and soars above the storm, and the peace of "shalom" that brings Your favor, Your friendship, and Your inward rest and tranquility.

Father, continue to draw my children into Your presence, and bring into their hearts all the joys that come from trusting in You, all the strength that comes from leaning on You, and all the delights that come from communing with You.

Kingdom Power

Promise

*God did not give us a spirit of timidity
or cowardice or fear, but [He has given us a spirit]
of power and of love and of sound judgment
and personal discipline [abilities that result in a calm,
well-balanced mind and self-control].*

2 Timothy 1:7 AMP

The kingdom of God is not in word but in power.

1 Corinthians 4:20 NKJV

Prayer

I thank You, God, for the power of Your kingdom—the power to change, transform, turn things upside down for the good, and make all things new in our hearts and lives. Thank You that Your ways are higher than our ways, Your plans better than our plans, and Your wisdom greater than our wisdom.

I pray that my children will always see life in the light and understanding of how You see things. May their eyes behold You and never forget what You've shown them. May they know Your mind and think Your thoughts. Teach them, Father, the ways of Your kingdom—the way of losing to gain, dying to live, becoming weak to find strength, possessing nothing yet making others rich, taking the lowly place in order to be lifted up, and forsaking what is temporary in order to inherit the things that will last forever.

May the power of Christ rest on us and His kingdom reign within us. May His love move us from what is superficial to what is genuine, what is fake to what is real, what is empty to what is abundant, and what is meaningless to what has eternal worth.

Unity

Promise

Come to Me, all you who labor and are heavy laden,
and I will give you rest.
Take My yoke upon you and learn from Me,
for I am gentle and lowly in heart,
and you will find rest for your souls.
For My yoke is easy and My burden is light.

Matthew 11:28–30 NKJV

Prayer

Thank You, Jesus, for calling my children, inviting them, and welcoming them to be united with You and joined to You—heart to heart, purpose to purpose, deep to deep, will to will, hand to hand, and love to love. I thank You for being the balancing point of their lives, and showing them that without You everything gets out of order and out of whack.

Thank You for being the God whose yoke is easy and burden is light. I pray that my children will know the release, the freedom, and the pleasant rest of being yoked to You. Teach them what it means to live with the mind of a servant, walk with a humble disposition, respond with a meek spirit, and reach out to others with a gentle heart.

I pray that my dear children will always trust in Your shed blood to cleanse them from all their sin, Your power to lift their burdens, and Your grace to meet the needs of each new day.

At the Heart of the Prayer

A key focus of each prayer to carry in your heart.

Sufficiency

I pray that the eyes of my children will remain wide open to see Your awesomeness. May they know how vast is Your greatness, how deep is Your love, how high are Your ways, how rich are Your treasures, how abundant are Your blessings, how full are Your joys, and how generous are Your gifts.

Fruitfulness

May my children's lives be blessed like the tree that is planted by rivers of water. May their roots go down deep into Your wisdom, their branches blossom with Your understanding, and their lives bring forth the peaceful fruits of righteousness.

Fullness

As I pray for my children today, I ask that they will know the height, breadth, length, and depth of Your abundant life. May they find the fulfillment of the deepest desires of their hearts—understanding why they are here and who You made them to be.

Access

I am so thankful today, Father, for the open gates of access into Your presence and the open arms of access into Your love. There is no end to the riches we find in You.

Kingdom Power

Father, teach my children the ways of Your kingdom— the way of losing to gain, dying to live, becoming weak to find strength, possessing nothing yet making others rich, taking the lowly place in order to be lifted up, and forsaking what is temporary in order to inherit the things that will last forever.

Unity

Thank You, Jesus, for calling my children, inviting them, and welcoming them to be united with You and joined to You—heart to heart, purpose to purpose, deep to deep, will to will, hand to hand, and love to love. I pray that my children will know the release, the freedom, and the pleasant rest of being yoked to You.

Section Nine

THE PRIVILEGE OF KNOWING GOD

The Privilege of Knowing God

We have not stopped praying for you since we first heard about you. We ask God to give you complete knowledge of His will and to give you spiritual wisdom and understanding. Then the way you live will always honor and please the Lord, and your lives will produce every kind of good fruit. All the while, you will grow as you learn to know God better and better.

Colossians 1:9–10 NLT

There is nothing greater in life than knowing God and His Son, Jesus Christ—this is our highest calling, greatest purpose, deepest love, richest treasure, and fullest joy. Above all, as you pray for your children, pray they will know Him—personally, fully, truly, and completely.

What an awesome privilege your children have been given to know God. This is why they were created—not just to hear about God, not just to learn about God, not just to read about God, not just to know about God, but to actually know God in reality and in truth.

Your children's hearts were made to be filled with Him, talk with Him, fellowship with Him, walk with Him, worship Him, and delight in Him. They were meant to know what He thinks, feel what He feels, and desire what He desires. That has always been God's plan for all of us—to know Him, enjoy Him, and glorify Him.

This section's promises focus on the following needs:

Companionship

Living Water

Legacy

Praise

Love

Goodness

Companionship

Promise

I will pray the Father, and He will give you another Helper, that He may abide with you forever—the Spirit of truth, whom the world cannot receive, because it neither sees Him nor knows Him; but you know Him, for He dwells with you and will be in you. I will not leave you orphans; I will come to you.

John 14:16–18 NKJV

Prayer

Jesus, You are so good to us. Thank You for not leaving us alone—for coming to us and being with us. Thank You for sending the Holy Spirit. Thank You for His presence, His power, His companionship, and His life.

I pray that my children will delight themselves in the sweet fellowship of the Holy Spirit—knowing His voice, having His peace, experiencing His joy. Thank You that Your Holy Spirit has come. Thank You that we are not like orphans. Thank You for sending someone to us—someone who will remain with us and be in us—someone who is exactly like You.

May my children know the Holy Spirit as their closest, dearest Friend—the One who is always there to encourage them, speak the truth to them, comfort and care for them, help and instruct them, listen to the cry of their hearts, pray for them, love them, and be with them forever.

Living Water

Promise

On the last and most important day of the feast,
Jesus stood and called out [in a loud voice],
"If anyone is thirsty, let him come to Me and drink!
He who believes in Me [who adheres to, trusts in, and
relies on Me], as the Scripture has said,
'From his innermost being will flow continually rivers
of living water.'"

John 7:37–38 AMP

Prayer

Lord Jesus, the promises You have given us are truly amazing, awesome, wondrous, and life-changing. What joys and wonders are ours when we believe in You and receive from You. I pray that my children will reach out for and receive everything You desire to give them.

In their spiritual thirst, may they come to You and drink. I pray that deep within their innermost beings will flow the rivers of Your Holy Spirit—rivers of grace, rivers of mercy, rivers of renewal, rivers of refreshing, and rivers of healing. May Your life bubble up within them, may Your praises spring up in their hearts, and may Your love flow out through them.

I pray that each one of them will abide in the "River of Your Delights." By faith, may they step into the flow and taste the freedom that the river of Your Holy Spirit can bring to their lives. May they wade out to where the water is ankle high, knee high, waist high, and then deep enough to swim.

Legacy

Promise

The godly are showered with blessings.
...We have happy memories of the godly.

Proverbs 10:6–7 NLT

Prayer

Father, thank You for blessing the lives of my children so they can be a blessing to others. Truly, Father, Your blessings upon them are more precious than the royal crowns worn on the heads of the kings and queens of this world. I pray that by Your grace and power, You will work within them all they will need to bring encouragement and enrichment to every life they touch.

Speak to them the soothing words that will heal hurting hearts, the wise words that will guide seeking hearts, the assuring words that will comfort grieving hearts, the accepting words that will embrace lonely hearts, the affirming words that will strengthen fearful hearts, and the life-giving words that will fill empty hearts.

I pray that through the testimony of their lives, my children will encourage others to know You better and love You more. May there be many who will say of them, "I thank God for you."

Praise

Promise

*Stand up and bless the L*ORD* your God Forever and ever!*
"Blessed be Your glorious name, which is exalted above
*all blessing and praise! You alone are the L*ORD*;*
You have made heaven, the heaven of heavens,
with all their host, the earth and everything on it,
the seas and all that is in them,
and You preserve them all.
The host of heaven worships You.

Nehemiah 9:5–6 NKJV

Prayer

I thank You, Lord, for this—above all Your blessings, You are the greatest blessing of all; above all Your gifts, You are the greatest gift of all; and above all Your joys, You are the greatest joy of all!

Lord, higher than what You give, You are the Giver; higher than what You create, You are the Creator; higher than what You heal, You are the Healer; higher than what has been redeemed, You are the Redeemer. To have You is to have everything! Thank You for all You are to each of us.

Father, I pray that my children will worship You and only You. Fill their hearts with hallelujahs. May they sing unto You psalms, hymns, and spiritual songs. May their voices be filled with rejoicing, their tongues proclaim Your praise, and their hearts be filled with thanksgiving. May they walk in the excitement of Your presence, the wonder of Your works, the freedom of Your purity, and the greatness of Your power. May You be their daily delight, as well as the joy and rejoicing of their hearts.

Love

Promise

Beloved, let us love one another,
for love is of God; and everyone who loves is born of
God and knows God. He who does not love does not
know God, for God is love.
...We have known and believed the love that God
has for us. God is love, and he who abides in love
abides in God, and God in him.

I John 4:7–8,16 NKJV

Prayer

I thank You, Lord, for being the essence of what love means—knowing You is to know love, receiving You is to receive love, having You is to have love, expressing You is to express love. Thank You that Your love will never wear out, fade out, burn out, or tire out. I pray that Your love will be poured into the lives of my children so that they will know the meaning of love at its deepest level.

I pray that my children will be lovers of God, and that through them others will come to know Your love. May Your love flood their hearts, fill their minds, move their wills, form their words, motivate their actions, and shape their character. May they speak the truth in love, walk in love, and abide in love.

I pray that my children will know the freedom that love brings to their lives. May they come to know for themselves and extend to others, Your unconditional love—without partiality, without limitations, and without measure. Thank You for extending Your love to each of us and for the privilege of being receivers of that love.

Goodness

Promise

Know that the L<small>ORD</small>, He is God; It is He who has made
us, and not we ourselves; we are His people and
the sheep of His pasture. Enter into His gates with
thanksgiving, and into His courts with praise.
Be thankful to Him, and bless His name.
For the L<small>ORD</small> is good; His mercy is everlasting,
and His truth endures to all generations.

Psalm 100:3–5 NKJV

Prayer

Thank You, Heavenly Father, for being a good God and doing good things for us, to us, and in us. I thank You that You are good to my children and Your eye is on every detail of their lives. Thank You that no one could ever be as good to them as You are!

Keep my children in the center of Your love and Your designed purpose, assuring them that You are working all things together for their good, and fitting them into Your perfect plan.

May the goodness of Your light shine upon them, the goodness of Your grace be with them, and the goodness of Your love be in them. Through Your goodness, may they experience all the delights of abiding in Your presence—the embrace of Your mercies, the warmth of Your nearness, the pleasure of Your fellowship, the joy of Your friendship, the peace of Your person, the rest of Your comfort, and the favor of Your smile.

At the Heart of the Prayer

A key focus of each prayer to carry in your heart.

Companionship

I pray that my children will delight themselves in the sweet fellowship of the Holy Spirit—knowing His voice, having His peace, and experiencing His joy. Thank You that the Holy Spirit has come, not only to be with them, but to be in them.

Living Water

In their spiritual thirst, may they come to You and drink. I pray that deep within their innermost beings will flow the rivers of Your Holy Spirit—rivers of grace, rivers of mercy, rivers of renewal, rivers of refreshing, and rivers of healing

Legacy

I pray that through the testimony of their lives, my children will encourage others to know You better and love You more. May there be many who will say of them, "I thank God for you."

Praise

Father, I pray that my children will worship You and only You. Fill their hearts with hallelujahs. May they sing unto You psalms, hymns, and spiritual songs. May their voices be filled with rejoicing and their tongues proclaim Your praise.

Love

Father, may Your love flood my children's hearts, fill their minds, move their wills, form their words, motivate their actions, and shape their character.

Goodness

Thank You that no one could ever be as good to my children as You are! Keep them in the center of Your love and Your designed purpose, assuring them that You are working all things together for their good, and fitting them into Your perfect plan.

Section Ten

SPIRITUAL GROWTH

Spiritual Growth

The righteous shall flourish like a palm tree, He shall grow like a cedar in Lebanon. Those who are planted in the house of the LORD shall flourish in the courts of our God. They shall still bear fruit in old age; they shall be fresh and flourishing.
Psalm 92:12–14 NKJV

What an awesome privilege and blessing it is to be the parent of a newborn baby. There are no words to describe the joy a new life brings to a family. The heart's desire of every parent should be to see each child grow and mature physically and spiritually, in wisdom, and in all God has for their lives.

Each parent has an important contribution to make in the development of a child's life. As a parent you can sow the seeds of God's Word into the hearts of your children. You can also pray that each seed will take deep root, be nourished by the showers of God's blessing, bathed with the sunshine of His grace and love, and become abundantly fruitful in every aspect of life.

This section's promises focus on the following needs:

Generosity

Prayer

Newness of Life

Knowing You

So Great Salvation

The Blessing of the Lord

Generosity

Promise

The Lord God is a sun and shield;
the Lord bestows grace and favor and honor;
no good thing will He withhold from those
who walk uprightly.

Psalm 84:11 AMP

Prayer

Heavenly Father, thank You for being so kind, so gracious, and so generous. Thank You for giving and giving and giving again. Thank You for Your generosity extended to us through Your abundant grace and favor. I ask that the brilliance of Your light will shine upon the lives of my children, and that You will be to them the sunshine of each day. As the sun rises in the east, so may the light of Your generous love greet them each morning.

May You be the shield that is about them, keeping them safe from every foe that wants to steal their peace, rob them of their joy, and keep them from Your blessings. I pray against every lie that would tell them You can't be trusted.

I ask that the hearts of my children will rest in Your care, being fully persuaded that You will hold back nothing from them that is good and right.

Prayer

Promise

*I say to you, ask, and it will be given to you;
seek, and you will find; knock, and it will be opened
to you. For everyone who asks receives, and he who
seeks finds, and to him who knocks it will be opened.*

Luke 11:9–10 NKJV

Prayer

What a glorious privilege You have given me, Father—the invitation to come freely into Your presence, placing my requests before You, asking You to meet my children's needs, and sharing the deepest desires of my heart. Thank You for allowing me to come before You anytime, anywhere, with anything I need to ask.

My deep desire is that my children would be people of prayer. Teach them how to pray, guide them when they pray, and encourage them as they pray. May they learn to come boldly before You, lean confidently upon You, wait patiently for You, listen carefully to You, hear clearly from You, open their hearts to You, and receive from You all they need.

Encourage them to knock because the door will be opened, ask because they will receive, and seek because they will find. May they be free of any doubt or uncertainty regarding Your will. May they pray with full assurance, unfettered boldness, and confident faith, knowing that You hear their prayers and answer them.

Newness of Life

Promise

Do not remember the former things,
or ponder the things of the past.
Listen carefully, I am about to do a new thing,
now it will spring forth; will you not be aware of it?
I will even put a road in the wilderness,
rivers in the desert.

Isaiah 43:18–19 AMP

Prayer

Lord, thank You for what You came to do and for successfully carrying that out in the lives of those who put their trust in You. How wonderful it is to know You have come to make us new. Thank You for the new things You want to do in the lives of my children—giving them life, bringing them hope, building their faith, and conforming them to Your image and likeness.

Keep their hearts full of expectancy as they reach out for new things in Your kingdom, keep their spiritual lives vibrant as they walk down new paths in Your will keep their vision ever expanding as they climb new heights by Your grace. I ask that each of their relationships with You will be always fresh and overflowing.

May their eyes be fixed on what is ahead rather than what is past. May new joys, new vision, and the new adventures that come from seeing You work Your wonders spring forth in their lives. Make a way for them through every wilderness, bring them to Your refreshing rivers, and be to them their heart's delight.

Knowing You

Promise

*"Let the one who boasts boast in this, that he
understands and knows Me
[and acknowledges Me and honors Me as God and
recognizes without any doubt],
that I am the LORD who practices lovingkindness,
justice and righteousness on the earth,
for in these things I delight," says the LORD.*

Jeremiah 9:24 AMP

Prayer

Father, there is nothing greater than to know You. You are greater than all and transcend all things. Thank You for sending Your only begotten Son to give His life, shed His precious blood, and open the way for us to come into Your presence. May my children glory in this one thing, that they know You as their one true God.

May their fellowship with You grow sweeter and sweeter, their love for You grow deeper and deeper, their walk with You grow more and more precious, and their knowledge of You grow with every passing year. May they thrive in Your nearness, delight in Your presence, celebrate Your goodness, rejoice in Your greatness, and rest in Your love.

May they see and know Your heart. May they always be assured that You care greatly about them and for them. May they recognize Your character and understand Your ways. May they joyously and worshipfully say, "You are my God."

So Great Salvation

Promise

He saved us, through the washing of regeneration and renewing of the Holy Spirit, whom He poured out on us abundantly through Jesus Christ our Savior, that having been justified by His grace we should become heirs according to the hope of eternal life.

Jeremiah 9:24 AMP

Prayer

Thank You, Father, for Your great salvation so full and free. To lose You is to lose all things, but to have You is to gain all things. Thank You for forgiving our sins— washing us clean, changing us from within, renewing us by Your Holy Spirit, and assuring us of our hope of heaven.

May "Salvation" be the banner that flies over the hearts of my children. May its proclamation be upon their lips, and its fruit be within their lives. May the joys of their salvation grow greater with each new day. May the hope of heaven always go before them through life, as they make choices, as they give, and as they serve.

May they never look back, turn back, or be held back as they run their race, keeping their eyes upon the heavenly prize and awaiting their eternal inheritance as joint-heirs of Jesus Christ. Help them to make each day count for eternity.

The Blessing of the Lord

Promise

*The L*ORD *spoke to Moses, saying: "Speak to Aaron and his sons, saying, 'This is the way you shall bless the children of Israel. Say to them: "The L*ORD *bless you and keep you; The L*ORD *make His face shine upon you, and be gracious to you; The L*ORD *lift up His countenance upon you, and give you peace.'"*

Numbers 6:22–27 NKJV

Prayer

Father, my heart is full of praise and gratitude to You for blessing me with the gift of these beautiful children. I want to say, over and over again, "Thank You so much!" Your blessings leave me in awe. You have enriched my life in more ways than I could ever imagine.

Your blessing means everything. My deep desire is that my children will be blessed of the Lord. May the fullness of Your blessing be upon them. As Aaron spoke Your blessing over the people of Israel, so I speak Your blessing over my children today.

"Father, bless my children with Your favor and kindness and keep them by Your power and strength. May Your face shine upon them with the light of Your radiant love; may they know the abundant riches of Your amazing grace; may You look down upon them with the smile of Your countenance; may You shield their hearts and minds with Your perfect peace that passes all understanding. Amen!"

At the Heart of the Prayer

A key focus of each prayer to carry in your heart.

Generosity

Heavenly Father, thank You for being so kind, so gracious, and so generous. Thank You for giving and giving and giving again. I ask that the hearts of my children will rest in Your care, being fully persuaded that You will hold back nothing from them that is good and right.

Prayer

My deep desire is that my children would be people of prayer. Teach them how to pray, guide them when they pray, and encourage them as they pray.

Newness of Life

I ask that each of my children's relationships with You will be always fresh and overflowing. May their eyes be fixed on what is ahead rather than what is past. May new joys, new vision, and the new adventures that come from seeing You work Your wonders spring forth in their lives.

Knowing You

May my children glory in this one thing, that they know You as their one true God. May their fellowship with You grow sweeter and sweeter, their love for You grow deeper and deeper, their walk with You grow more and more precious, and their knowledge of You grow with every passing year.

So Great Salvation

Father, may "Salvation" be the banner that flies over the hearts of my children. May its proclamation be upon their lips and its fruit be within their lives.

The Blessing of the Lord

Your blessing means everything. My deep desire is that my children will be blessed of the Lord. May the fullness of Your blessing be upon them.

Lord, I place my children into Your hands.
I commit them to Your care and keeping.
Thank You for being their provider, their keeper, their
helper, and their shepherd.
Thank You for Your promise to lead them,
nurture them, abide with them,
and follow after them with goodness
and mercy all the days of their lives.

DaySpring

LIVE YOUR FAITH

Dear Friend,

This book was prayerfully crafted with you, the reader, in mind—every word, every sentence, every page—was thoughtfully written, designed, and packaged to encourage you...right where you are this very moment. At DaySpring, our vision is to see every person experience the life-changing message of God's love. So, as we worked through rough drafts, design changes, edits and details, we prayed for you to deeply experience His unfailing love, indescribable peace, and pure joy. It is our sincere hope that through these Truth-filled pages your heart will be blessed, knowing that God cares about you—your desires and disappointments, your challenges and dreams.

He knows. He cares. He loves you unconditionally.

BLESSINGS!
THE DAYSPRING BOOK TEAM

Additional copies of this book and
other DaySpring titles can be purchased
at fine bookstores everywhere.
Order online at <u>dayspring.com</u>
or
by phone at 1-877-751-4347